Punctuation
Book three

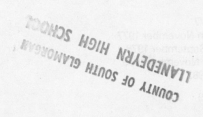

T. G. Ledgard M.A.

Deputy Headmaster, Sheldon School,
Chippenham

Cassell
London

CASSELL LTD.
Greycoat House, 10 Greycoat Place
London SW1P 1SB

An affiliate of Macmillan Publishing Co. Inc.
New York

First published 1977
Second impression November 1977
Third impression September 1978
Fourth impression November 1979
Fifth impression 1982

ISBN 0 304 29773 9

Printed in Hong Kong by Colorcraft Ltd

Contents

Introduction

For some time now the emphasis in the teaching of written English has been on free personal expression and creative writing. While these must be the most worthwhile of all written English activities, they have been pursued in many cases at the expense of good handwriting, careful spelling and correct punctuation. Many adults—including parents, employers and heads of English departments in Secondary schools—feel that today's pupils do not receive the basic grounding in mechanical accuracy which is necessary for good written English.

This series of four books, a systematic punctuation course designed for regular use in the Secondary (or Middle) school, is intended to meet a need which will become increasingly obvious as the pendulum swings back towards a greater concern for correct English.

The books are written in the simplest possible way, avoiding all but the most common and easily understood grammatical terms, yet they cover all punctuation marks in all their usages. The series is so arranged that, if desired, 'Punctuation 1' could be used for first years in Secondary schools, 'Punctuation 2' for second years, and so on. There are carefully compiled and graded exercises on all punctuation marks as well as a large number of revision exercises.

Correct punctuation is as important as correct spelling and easily legible handwriting. Pupils who are taken through this series in a systematic way will gain a thorough understanding of something that is an essential element of good written English.

Comma

In Book 1 we said that the COMMA (,) was used in a number of different ways, but always to separate words or groups of words from each other. You learned how to use it between items in a list and to mark off a term of address. We have also seen that it is often used before or after Direct Speech. We shall now look at the other uses of the comma.

A pair of commas to mark off groups of words which are not absolutely necessary

Very often a sentence will contain a word or a group of words which should be marked off from the rest of the sentence. This is because the words are not absolutely necessary to the meaning; the sentence would still make perfectly good sense without them. To mark off this word or group of words we use a pair of commas.

Pairs of commas are used round words or groups of words which must be marked off from the rest of the sentence because they are not absolutely necessary to the meaning.

For example:

Dad, lying in the bath, got his toe stuck in the tap.

In this sentence *lying in the bath* is not absolutely necessary to the meaning; the sentence still makes perfectly good sense without these words. So we mark them off from the rest of the sentence with a pair of commas.

There are four sorts of words or groups of words which are marked off from the rest of the sentence with a pair of commas in this way. The first three are groups of words all of which

* are not absolutely necessary to the meaning of the sentence,
* tell us more about someone or something,
* always come immediately before or after the person or thing they describe.

A. The first is a group of words which is actually another way of describing someone or something, often the name.

Example: *Our English teacher, Mr. Hancock, is the best in the school.*

In this sentence, *Mr. Hancock* is another way of describing *Our English teacher*. It is, in fact, his name. The words, *Mr. Hancock*, are not absolutely necessary. If they were left out, the sentence would read

Our English teacher is the best in the school.

This would make perfectly good sense. So we use commas to mark off the words, *Mr. Hancock*.

Exercise 1:

Each of the sentences below contains a group of words which is another way of describing what goes immediately before it. Write out each sentence, underlining the group of words and surrounding it with a pair of commas.

Example: *Mrs. Siddons the village gossip was leaning on the fence.*
becomes *Mrs. Siddons, the village gossip, was leaning on the fence.*

(a) Paris the capital of France is a beautiful city.
(b) Mrs. Vines our neighbour willingly agreed to feed our hens.
(c) Mr. Stamp the postman knocked on the door.
(d) Treasure Island a most exciting story is my favourite book.
(e) The Skylark the oldest boat in the harbour was sunk by the storm.
(f) I think that the cane a cruel instrument should be made illegal.
(g) Noddy saw Mr. Plod the policeman coming up the street.
(h) Toby my friend is an excellent shot with an air rifle.
(i) I do not wish my daughter Jane to see your son again.
(j) I am complaining about today's school dinner a meal fit only for starving animals to the Headmaster.

Exercise 2:

Do as you did in exercise 1 but this time do not underline the groups of words; just surround them with a pair of commas.

(a) Mr. Bunn the baker makes lovely bread.
(b) He kept pigs very clean animals as well as hens.
(c) They had nowhere to live when their house a dangerous slum was pulled down by the council.
(d) The school was surprised when Jerry an unpopular boy was made a prefect.
(e) The garden a jungle of weeds was full of mice, voles and hedgehogs.
(f) My mother wrote a letter to Mr. Green my teacher to explain why I had not done my homework.
(g) The workers came out on strike when Bill their mate was unfairly given the sack.
(h) Haggis the stuffed stomach of a sheep is the national dish of the Scots.

(i)   Ronnie Wilson the star of the team played another brilliant game.

(j)   The homework a very difficult exercise was not done correctly by anyone.

B. The second is a group of words which usually (though not always) begins with a word ending in *-ing* or *-ed*.

We have already seen this example:

> *Dad, lying in the bath, got his toe stuck in the tap.*

The words, *lying in the bath*, are not absolutely necessary to the meaning of the sentence so we mark them off with a pair of commas.

We could equally well place *lying in the bath* before *Dad*, like this:

> *Lying in the bath, Dad got his toe stuck in the tap.*

Notice that, when a group of words which should be surrounded by a pair of commas begins a sentence, it does not need the first comma. In the same way, such a group of words at the end of a sentence has a full stop (or question mark or exclamation mark) instead of the second comma, e.g.

> *The person who got his toe stuck in the tap was Dad, lying in the bath.*

Exercise 3:

Each of the sentences below contains a group of words, beginning with a word ending in *-ing* or *-ed*, which tells us more about someone or something. Write out each sentence, underlining the group of words and surrounding it with a pair of commas. Remember that, if the group of words comes at the beginning of a sentence, you will not need the first comma; if it comes at the end of a sentence, the second comma will become the full stop (or question mark or exclamation mark).

Example: *Shutting her eyes she counted to ten.*
becomes *Shutting her eyes, she counted to ten.*

(a) Singing loudly she began to wash the dishes.
(b) Sitting up in Granny's bed the wolf looked greedily at Little Red Riding Hood.
(c) Dressed in his best suit Richard went off happily to his first morning at work.
(d) Having taken an enormous mouthful he began to eat with his mouth open.
(e) Last night Sheila walking in her sleep fell downstairs.
(f) The referee feeling he ought to be strict sent Dixon off the field.
(g) The walkers all thoroughly exhausted collapsed on the ground.
(h) Balancing very carefully the acrobat began to walk across the wire.
(i) Losing his temper Mr. Watson shouted at the class.
(j) Having dropped the brick on his foot he grunted in pain.

Exercise 4:

Do as you did in exercise 3 but this time do not underline the groups of words.

(a) Feeling rather shaky he got out of bed and wobbled to the door.
(b) Aunt Joan died last month loved by all who knew her.
(c) She strolled happily through the grass singing as she went.
(d) While shepherds watched their flocks by night all seated on the ground the Angel of the Lord came down.
(e) He slammed the car door and waving happily to us all drove off down the road.

(f)   The teacher saying that it hurt him to do it gave me two strokes of the cane.

(g)   The chestnuts falling out of the tree were collected by the boys below.

(h)   Chuckling quietly to himself my father went upstairs.

(i)   Mary lay on the bed sobbing her heart out.

(j)   The happy couple left the church smiling broadly and covered in confetti.

C. The third is a group of words which begins with a word like *who, which, whose,* etc.

Example: *My mother, who is a very gentle person, never loses her temper.*

In this sentence *who is a very gentle person* is marked off with commas. It is a group of words beginning with *who* and telling us more about someone, *my mother;* but it is not absolutely necessary to the meaning of the sentence.

Exercise 5:

Each of the sentences below contains a group of words telling us more about someone or something and beginning with *who, which, whose,* etc. Write out each sentence, underlining the group of words and surrounding it with commas. Remember that, if the group of words comes at the end of a sentence, the second comma will become the full stop (or question mark or exclamation mark).

Example: *Mary Ann who was the cleverest girl in the class knew all the answers.*
becomes *Mary Ann, who was the cleverest girl in the class, knew all the answers.*

(a)   Our post office which is run by Mrs. Hicks sells everything from toothpaste to tomatoes.

(b) I want you all to stand up when Mr. Flowers who is coming to talk to you enters the classroom.

(c) I am taking this book which is the most boring I have ever read back to the library tomorrow.

(d) Our dog who is very fierce bit the milkman yesterday.

(e) Your blue cup which was already cracked broke when I dropped it.

(f) I have written to thank my aunt with whom I stayed last weekend.

(g) I saw Fred whose bicycle you have borrowed and he says he wants it back immediately.

(h) My bath for which there was only cold water was most unpleasant.

(i) The Headmaster who is a kind man patted me on the head and told me to behave myself.

(j) He went to fill his pen which had run out of ink.

Exercise 6:

Do as you did in exercise 5 but this time do not underline the groups of words.

(a) The magistrate warned Fred who was shouting to behave himself.

(b) I collected my dress which I had taken to be cleaned.

(c) After Auld Lang Syne which we sang at midnight we all went to bed.

(d) Their goldfish which they had looked after for years died last week.

(e) Cornwall where my grandfather lives is a beautiful part of the country.

(f) Tessie wondered if her project over which she had spent so long would be good enough.

(g) The two hitch-hikers were given a ride all the way to London for which they were very grateful.

(h) I saw the manager who told me to come back this afternoon.

(i)   Do you know North Wales where we went for our holiday last year?

(j)   The river Trent by the side of which we were camping looked dangerously swollen.

For this kind of group of words (telling us more about someone or something and beginning with *who*, *which*, *whose*, etc.) it is most important that you should remember the phrase, **not absolutely necessary**. Sometimes such a group of words **is** absolutely necessary to the meaning. When this is the case, we cannot hide it away between a pair of commas. For example:

I have never met a person who always tells the truth.

In this sentence the group of words, *who always tells the truth*, is absolutely necessary. If we leave it out, we would have *I have never met a person.*, which is clearly nonsense.

So we can say that we mark off a group of words with the commas only if it is **not absolutely necessary** to the sentence. Here is another example:

The man who brought his umbrella is very sensible.

In this sentence *who brought his umbrella* is absolutely necessary. Without this group of words we should not know which man was meant. So there are no commas.

But if the sentence had been

Mr. Sparks, who brought his umbrella, is very sensible.

then we know who is meant as soon as we read the words, *Mr. Sparks*. The words, *who brought his umbrella*, are not absolutely necessary and so are marked off with a pair of commas.

So we can say that, if we **know** who or what is meant without the describing group of words, then the group of words is not absolutely necessary. It is therefore marked off with a pair of commas.

If we **do not know** who or what is meant until we read the describing group of words, then we cannot possibly hide them away between a pair of commas. The describing words are necessary to the sentence and so must not be marked off with commas.

Exercise 7:

Each of the sentences below contains a group of words telling us more about someone or something and beginning with *who, which, whose,* etc. Some of the describing groups of words are absolutely necessary and some are not. If they **are** necessary, write out the sentence exactly as it is without adding any commas. If they are **not absolutely necessary**, add commas and underline the describing group of words.

Examples: *Will the boy who threw that piece of chalk own up at once?* is written out exactly as it is, but *David Jones who threw that piece of chalk will be punished.* becomes *David Jones, who threw that piece of chalk, will be punished.*

(a) Will the person who parked a red sports car in front of my garage door please remove it at once?
(b) Mrs. Shield who parked her car on a pedestrian crossing was fined £10.
(c) Is there anybody here who can help me?
(d) The president of the club to whom I spoke was very friendly.
(e) The man to whom I was speaking turned out to be wanted by the police.
(f) The fish which he caught were so small that he threw them back.
(g) The tall man in the dark suit who had been sitting quietly at the back of the hall got quickly to his feet.
(h) I have not yet spoken to Mrs. Winchester who is our new Headmistress.

(i)   Can you tell me if this is the road which leads to the motorway?

(j)   He threw a tired punch at his opponent who side-stepped neatly.

Quite often a group of words of the kind we learned about on page 8 is also necessary to the sentence. For example, in this sentence,

Would the lady wearing the red coat please stand up?

wearing the red coat is necessary to the meaning. If it were left out, we should not know which lady was meant.

Sometimes, even if we know who or what is meant, a group of words like this may still be necessary. It may contain words absolutely necessary to the meaning of the sentence, e.g. *I heard you singing in the bath*. We could not leave out *singing in the bath* without altering what the sentence meant, so we do not hide the words away between a pair of commas.

In cases like these, where the group of words **is** absolutely necessary, we follow the same rule that we learned on page 12; only if the group of words is **not absolutely necessary**, do we mark it off with a pair of commas.

Exercise 8:

In the sentences below there are describing groups of words of all the three types we have learned so far in this book. Place commas around those which are not absolutely necessary to the sentence. (You no longer need to underline anything.) Do not place commas around describing groups of words which **are** necessary.

Example: *Sarah's doll which is called Jane has been eaten by the dog.*
becomes *Sarah's doll, which is called Jane, has been eaten by the dog.*

(a) She thought that Sammy the leader of the group had rather a squeaky voice.

(b) Her boyfriend who was very stupid was very handsome.

(c) Charles who was climbing through his bedroom window was seen by Uncle Percy.

(d) Uncle Percy said that the person who climbed into the house through a bedroom window had woken him up.

(e) Barking loudly Bonzo chased the milkman back to his van.

(f) She looked up and was surprised to see a helicopter hovering above her.

(g) The man who had been knocked down struggled to his feet while the other man ran away.

(h) Margaret who was actually trembling with fear said she had always been frightened of going to the dentist.

(i) He looked hopelessly at his food a few grey pieces of meat in a sea of thin gravy.

(j) A policeman to whom we spoke told us the way to the zoo.

D. Fourthly, there are a few single words or very short groups of words which are usually marked off with commas. These are:

however   meanwhile   by the way   well
without doubt   moreover   nevertheless

and certain other words.

There is no rule to tell you when these words should be marked off with commas. But usually they need to be followed by a comma if they come at the beginning of a sentence, e.g.

However, he was more successful with his next shot.

If they come in the middle or at the end of a sentence, they are usually marked off with commas, but not always. It is up to you to decide whether you think you need a pause before and after the word or group of words concerned. For example, you could have either

The chair had, meanwhile, been mended.
or *The chair had meanwhile been mended.*

Exercise 9:

Write out the following sentences, adding commas where you feel it is necessary.

Example: *Well it was a difficult decision to make.*
becomes *Well, it was a difficult decision to make.*

(a) Mrs. Jones had however brought enough sandwiches for us all.
(b) By the way do you know Michael Jackson?
(c) It was without doubt the worst food I had ever tasted.
(d) Moreover he then lit a pipe and filled the room with foul-smelling smoke.
(e) He was nevertheless an intelligent person.
(f) Well I need hardly tell you how surprised I was.
(g) She knitted busily meanwhile.
(h) I wonder by the way if you would be good enough to help me push my car.
(i) They agreed to do it however.
(j) We shall meet you again no doubt.

Commas marking off groups of words beginning with *when, after,* etc.

As a general rule a comma is used after groups of words beginning with *when, after, before, until, while, since, if, unless, although, though, because* (and certain other words) if these groups of words begin a sentence, e.g.

If you buy me a new dress, I shall come to the party.

A pair of commas is used around groups of words

beginning with *when, after,* etc. if they come in the middle of a sentence, e.g.

She said that, if he bought her a new dress, she would go to the party.

No commas are necessary if the group of words comes at the end of the sentence, e.g.

I shall come to the party if you buy me a new dress.

Groups of words beginning with *when, after*, etc. are marked off with commas when they come at the beginning or in the middle of a sentence.

Exercise 10:

Each of the following sentences contains a group of words beginning with *when, after,* etc. Write out each sentence, adding commas where necessary. Some of the sentences will not need any commas.

Example: *When it stopped raining the sun came out.* becomes *When it stopped raining, the sun came out.*

(a)   If you feel ill you must stay in bed.
(b)   He says that if he is found guilty he will not pay the fine.
(c)   The match will take place if there is no more rain.
(d)   The family went away for a fortnight when the harvest was finished.
(e)   When the harvest was finished the family went away for a fortnight.
(f)   Tom went to the shops although he had been told to go straight home.
(g)   She thought that after she had finished her work she would go for a walk.
(h)   Unless you stop it I shall tell my father.
(i)   I shall tell my father unless you stop it.
(j)   Although he was short and fat Helen loved him dearly.

Exercise 11:

Do as you did in exercise 10.

(a) They could not understand why Mr. Hanson did not put his foot on the brake.

(b) Why Mr. Hanson did not put his foot on the brake they could not understand.

(c) The teacher said that because Ann had not worked she would not pass her exam.

(d) Whether we shall have a full team is doubtful.

(e) When the alarm went the building was cleared instantly.

(f) Bob was not sure whether to go back or go on.

(g) Sally said that although it was expensive she would go to the concert.

(h) He knew that even if he had had a map he would still have got lost.

(i) Your father never comes in from the garden until it is quite dark.

(j) Hilary knew that unless she stopped crying immediately her eyes would still be red and swollen when Edmund arrived.

Other uses of the comma

In addresses

A comma is used at the end of each line when you are writing an address (the last line ends in a full stop), e.g.

> *Miss E. N. Jenkins,*
> *21 Willow Walk,*
> *Petworth,*
> *Sussex.*

This way of punctuating addresses, placing a comma at the end of each line except the last, is still the most widely used. However, a new method is becoming more popular, especially in the world of commerce. This is to leave out commas at the end of each line.

It does not matter which rule you follow so long as you always do the same thing.

In letters

A comma is used after *Dear* _____, e.g. *Dear Sir*, or *Dear Emily*,.

A comma is also used after the final greeting, whether it is *Yours sincerely*, or *Yours faithfully*, or *With best wishes*, or *With love*,.

In dates

A comma is used when writing dates. It is placed between the day of the week (*Monday*), the day of the month (*18th October*) and the year (*1976*), e.g. *Monday, 18th October, 1976* or *18th October, 1976* or *Monday, 18th October*.

In numbers

A comma is used if there are more than three figures in a number. To write a million in figures, for example, we write *1,000,000*. In other words, we place a comma before every group of three figures, starting from the right, e.g. *19,276* or *27,389,441*.

Exercise 12:

Write out the words and figures below, adding commas where necessary. Set out correctly those which are addresses, not forgetting to add a full stop at the very end.

Example: *Mr. J. Woodman 5 Robin Way Exeter* becomes

> *Mr. J. Woodman,*
> *5 Robin Way,*
> *Exeter.*

(a) 3rd March 1947
(b) 5682
(c) Miss J. Brodie 21 Cliff Walk Aberdeen
(d) Tuesday 7th October 1972

(e)   The Personnel Officer J. B. King Ltd. Brislington
      Bristol
(f)   Dr. M. Nott 7 High Street Kington Lancashire
(g)   1897532413
(h)   Saturday 21st July
(i)   27842
(j)   James Walker The Beeches Hazel Farm Road
      Burston Norfolk

Exercise 13:

Write out the following letter, adding commas where
necessary. It is a business letter so you must set it out
exactly as it is set out here. Do not add any other
punctuation (except for three full stops after *Yorkshire*,
1976 and *London*).

                              Shop Supplies Ltd.
                              Sheffield Road
                              Hampton
                              Yorkshire
                              23rd October 1976

The Manager
Phizz-Cold Ltd.
5 New Trading Estate
Islington
London

Dear Sir
   On Monday 11th October we received a delivery of
12500 bottles of your Phizz-Cold Orange (125 cases of
100 bottles each). I have already had 1100 bottles (11
cases) returned to me by my customers. All the returned
bottles are faulty in that the tops have not been
correctly sealed so that the orange drink has lost its
aeration. I should be grateful if you would arrange to
inspect the remaining 11400 bottles and to replace all
those that are faulty.
                     Yours faithfully
                     E. Rowbotham (Manager)

Full stop after abbreviations

An abbreviation is a shortened word. Sometimes a word is shortened to one letter (the first) and sometimes to a few letters, e.g.

U.K. (for *United Kingdom*)
Mr. (for *Mister*)

Whether the abbreviation is one letter or more, the rule is:

Each abbreviated word is followed by a full stop.

(IMPORTANT: see bottom of page 23.)

Most abbreviations, but not all, begin with capital letters. Probably the most commonly used are a person's initials, e.g. *J. H. Smith* (for *John Henry Smith*). Here are some other common abbreviations:

Mr. (*Mister*)
Mrs. (*Missis*)
Rd. (*Road*)
St. (*Street*)
Ave. (*Avenue*)
U.N.O. (*United Nations Organization*)
B.C. (*before Christ*)
A.D. (*anno domini=after the birth of Christ*)
R.S.P.C.A. (*Royal Society for the Prevention of Cruelty to Animals*)

a.m. (*ante meridiem= before noon*)
p.m. (*post meridiem= after noon*)
e.g. (*exempli gratia= for example*)
i.e. (*id est=that is*)
Ltd. (*Limited*)
etc. (*et cetera*)
no. (*number*)
lb. (*pound in weight*)
oz. (*ounce*)

Exceptions are some abbreviations of units of measurement, e.g. *cc* (*cubic centimetres*), *km* (*kilometres*), *kg* (*kilograms*). The full stop is also omitted from *p* (*pence*).

Placing a full stop after an abbreviation makes no difference to any other punctuation. You can often have a full stop followed immediately by another punctuation mark, e.g.

> *J. H. Smith, Esq.,*
> *7 Ringway Rd.,*
> *Melton.*

However, if an abbreviation comes at the end of a sentence, **do not put a second full stop**.

Exercise 14:

Write out the following sentences, adding a full stop after each abbreviated word. Set out addresses correctly, as above.

Example: *I have agreed to see Mrs Watkins tomorrow at 10 am.*
becomes *I have agreed to see Mrs. Watkins tomorrow at 10 a.m.*

(a) Betty King gives £5 to the RSPCA each year.

(b) In 55 BC Julius Caesar invaded Britain.

(c) Mr V Walter, 68 Dunkirk Rd, Wilmington.

(d) The name of her father's company is A C Holman Ltd.

(e) Dr D A Spitz, 1018 Amherst Rd, Pittsburg, Pennsylvania, USA.

(f) Why did you not weigh the parcel to see if it was more than 2 lbs?

(g) It is now possible to buy a number of excellent 50 cc machines, eg the Mo-Speed.

(h) P W Tidmarsh Esq, 82 Lime Ave, Pinehurst, Hants.

(i)   The MV Ocean Queen sailed from Southampton at precisely 11.18 am.

(j)   H Mills Esq, BA, Dip Ed, 12 Lake Dr, Trowbridge, Wilts.

Exercise 15:

For what does each of the following abbreviations stand?

(a) Mrs.	(b) B.B.C.	(c) M.P.
(d) U.S.S.R.	(e) B.C.	(f) C.I.D.
(g) cc.	(h) a.m.	(i) J.P.
(j) Messrs.	(k) Esq.	(l) S.O.S.
(m) U.N.E.S.C.O.	(n) etc.	(o) B.A.
(p) U.F.O.	(q) e.g.	(r) Mme.
(s) G.M.T.	(t) km.	

If you do not know any of the answers, you can look them up in a good dictionary.

Important

This way of punctuating abbreviations, placing a full stop after each abbreviated word, is still the most widely used. However, a new method is becoming more popular, especially in the world of commerce. This is **to leave out the full stops after abbreviations**.

It does not matter which rule you follow so long as you always do the same thing.

If you decide not to use full stops after abbreviations, then the ten sentences in exercise 14 are all correct as they are.

Revision exercises

Full stop, question mark, exclamation mark

(from Book 1)

Revision exercise 1:

Write out the following, adding only full stops, question marks and exclamation marks (and capital letters at the beginning of each sentence). You should have ten sentences when you have finished.

what are the effects of smoking cigarettes first, smoking cigarettes damages your health by making you short of breath and generally unfit there now also seems to be medical evidence that smoking can cause serious and sometimes fatal illness secondly, smoking dirties you and your surroundings people who smoke have a stale smell and rooms in which there has been smoking have an unpleasant atmosphere finally, smoking damages your pocket as well do people who smoke 20 cigarettes a day not realise that they are watching almost £200 a year go up in smoke so why do people smoke the only possible reason is because they think it is a sign of being grown-up how stupid

Comma placed between items in a list and comma used to mark off a term of address

(from Book 1)

Revision exercise 2:

Write out the following sentences, adding commas

where necessary. Do not add any other punctuation.

(a) They liked Frances because she was lively honest friendly and cheerful.
(b) I hope Miss Fletcher that you will arrive on time tomorrow.
(c) For the second night running that wretched owl hooted hooted and hooted from dusk to dawn.
(d) Goodnight ladies.
(e) We shall leave when your mother has made the sandwiches when you two have tidied your rooms and when I have got the car out.
(f) Nicholas you cannot possibly have spent all your money already.
(g) Jack walked up the garden path with a spade in one hand with a fork in the other with a trowel in his pocket and with a determination in his heart never to agree to do the gardening again.
(h) She was very pretty and at the end of five minutes he had managed to find out her name address and telephone number.
(i) You Barbara are a lazy thoughtless and dishonest girl.
(j) Vincent William and Michael the Headmaster wants to see you now.

Speech marks

(from Book 2)

Revision exercise 3:

Write out the following sentences, placing a pair of speech marks round any Direct Speech. If there is no Direct Speech, copy out the sentence exactly as it is, without any speech marks.

(a) The tickets are too expensive, said Barbara sadly.
(b) Your rabbit is not very tame, explained their father, because you keep on picking it up and dropping it.
(c) The sergeant shouted, Stand still!
(d) Mr. Pitts said, Can you help me?
(e) Mr. Pitts asked if I could help him.
(f) Anthony, said his father crossly, I will not have you eating like a pig.
(g) Please get us out! screamed the trapped miners desperately.
(h) The Queen ended by saying, I wish you all a very happy Christmas.
(i) The conjuror says that he is ready to start now.
(j) Why, the coach asked the keeper, did you not stop that goal?

Revision exercise 4:

Write out the following sentences, placing a pair of speech marks round any Direct Speech and adding any other punctuation that may be necessary. If there is no Direct Speech, punctuate the sentence correctly without, of course, adding any speech marks.

(a) Please can I have my comic asked the small boy
(b) She wondered whether she ought to pick the baby up or let it go on crying
(c) How asked Anna do you know that this is the right answer
(d) The Queen said off with her head
(e) The fiercest of all the dinosaurs explained the teacher was the tyrannosaurus
(f) The mechanic asked Sid what was wrong with his bike
(g) Hallelujah shouted the preacher
(h) Tina could not explain why she felt so miserable
(i) The pilot shouted bale out
(j) The manager said the worker would be dismissed
     (There are two ways of punctuating this sentence.)

Apostrophe used instead of the word *of*

(from Book 2)

Revision exercise 5:

Write out the sentences below, adding apostrophes where necessary. Some of the sentences may not need any apostrophes at all.

(a) The warders eyes stared suspiciously at the two prisoners as they stood in front of him.
(b) Shearwaters spend their time gliding over the waves.
(c) The rioters threw stones at the policemens helmets.
(d) The spectators were dazzled by the flashing of the soldiers swords in the sun as they marched by.
(e) Johns cold has cleared up and he is going to school tomorrow.
(f) That books cover has been damaged because of the carelessness of the pupils.
(g) Sports cars sometimes make their owners friends envious.
(h) Teachers do not like a pupils work to be full of mistakes.
(i) The pianists fingers flew over the keys.
(j) It is not always a good idea to marry the bosss daughter.

Apostrophe used to show that you have left out a letter or letters

(from Book 2)

Revision exercise 6:

Write out the following sentences, adding apostrophes where necessary.

(a)   I didnt mean to be rude so please dont be cross.
(b)   Shes very old but she wont let me help her in any way.
(c)   Its one o clock and Marys sleep-walking again.
(d)   This plates cracked and Im not going to eat off it.
(e)   I cant possibly come today but Ill gladly come tomorrow.
(f)   Well look after the car while youre away.
(g)   There they were, just leaning on their spades and talking.
(h)   Im afraid we shant see him again for some time.
(i)   Youre going to be sorry that you havent worked when you sit your exams.
(j)   Its a pity that your teapot has had its spout broken.

A pair of commas to mark off groups of words which are not absolutely necessary

Revision exercise 7 (this exercise can be done after you have worked through to page 7):

Each of the sentences below contains a group of words which is not absolutely necessary to the sentence and is another way (sometimes the actual name) of describing what goes immediately before it. Write out each sentence, surrounding the group of words with a pair of commas. Do not add any other punctuation.

Example: *Their usual bus driver Mr. Boggis was on holiday.*
becomes *Their usual bus driver, Mr. Boggis, was on holiday.*

(a)   He was unhappy because his girlfriend Katy Bolton had just left him.
(b)   Pluto the furthest planet from the sun was discovered in 1930.
(c)   She lent me a book Making Rag Dolls when I was ill.

(d) Starling Street a narrow and dirty lane was full of people.

(e) Miss Scotland Fiona Black will open the new supermarket tomorrow.

(f) The race a long one was easily won by George Biggs.

(g) My secretary Miss Thompson will make an appointment for you.

(h) April my favourite month has been very wet for some years now.

(i) The Liverpool team winners of the F.A. Cup returned in triumph to the city.

(j) For 50p the cost of a packet of cigarettes you can buy a good book.

Revision exercise 8 (page 9):

Each of the sentences below contains a group of words, beginning with a word ending in *-ing* or *-ed*, which tells us more about someone or something. Write out each sentence, surrounding the group of words with a pair of commas. Remember that, if the group of words comes at the beginning or the end of the sentence, one of the commas will not be necessary.

Example: *Blowing in the wind the washing dried in half an hour.*
becomes *Blowing in the wind, the washing dried in half an hour.*

(a) Panting heavily the fat policeman ran along the pavement.

(b) The dog kicked viciously by its master ran howling from the house.

(c) Arriving first at the accident Jean rang for the ambulance.

(d) The wheels spinning furiously sprayed the spectators with mud.

(e) Your letter received by me this morning was very welcome.

(f) The crocodile disappeared thrashing its tail in the water.

(g) She lay awake all night worrying about her exam.

(h) The swarm of bees buzzing loudly settled on a tree near the house.

(i) Talking at the tops of their voices the girls walked along the road.

(j) Australia often said to be the largest island in the world can also be called the smallest continent.

Revision exercise 9 (page 11):

Each of the sentences below contains a group of words telling us more about someone or something and beginning with *who*, *which*, *whose*, etc. Write out each sentence, surrounding the group of words with commas. Remember that, if the group of words comes at the end of the sentence, the second comma will become the full stop (or question mark or exclamation mark).

Example: *Mr. Clark's Ford which he drives to work each day is very old.*
becomes *Mr. Clark's Ford, which he drives to work each day, is very old.*

(a) My letter which I posted last weekend had obviously not arrived.

(b) Mr. Sayers who is our neighbour is very keen on model aeroplanes.

(c) Do you know Jim Dingle who has the farm next to ours?

(d) Old Sam who has been a thief for years is really going straight now.

(e) Ellen's party to which you are all invited starts at 8 o'clock.

(f) The manager sacked Ted Mills whom he employed last year.

(g) He looked sadly at his bike which had been quite crushed by the lorry.

(h)   He proudly handed in his project on which he had
       worked for half a term.
(i)   Martin Dicks for whom you are taking the blame
       will not thank you for it.
(j)   James has gone to see Mr. Letts whose car he is
       hoping to buy.

Revision exercise 10 (page 15):

In the sentences below there are describing groups of
words of the three types introduced on pages 6, 8 and
10. Place commas around those which are not
absolutely necessary to the sentence. Some of the
sentences (those in which the describing groups of
words **are** necessary) you will need to write out exactly
as they are, without adding commas.

Example: *The tree which has died is an elm.* would be
written out exactly as it is because *which has died is*
necessary to the sentence.

(a)   The first person to reach the South Pole was
       Amundsen the Norwegian explorer.
(b)   Edgar James who was playing at full back had a
       magnificent game.
(c)   Dick Sims was a boy who never gave up.
(d)   The tall man waving his hand is my father.
(e)   The librarian Miss Gunge asked Carol to leave the
       library.
(f)   Down the street strode Mr. Wright swinging his
       arms like a soldier.
(g)   He did not commit the murder for which he was
       hanged.
(h)   Father was dismayed to find that his hair of which
       he was very proud was beginning to turn grey.
(i)   Any pupil who fails to do this homework will be
       punished.
(j)   Man the hunter came long before Man the farmer.

Revision exercise 11 (page 16):

In the sentences below there are single words like *however* and short groups of words like *by the way* which usually need to be marked off with a pair of commas. Write out each sentence, adding commas where you feel it is necessary. Do not add any other punctuation.

Example: *By the way where has John gone?*
becomes *By the way, where has John gone?*

(a) The traffic warden did not however give her a parking ticket.
(b) Nevertheless they did as they were told.
(c) He asked by the way if he could come and see you tonight.
(d) She was without doubt the best nurse in the hospital.
(e) In other words he felt ashamed of himself.
(f) Moreover it was a horrible day of wind and rain.
(g) They played cards and talked quietly meanwhile.
(h) Tomorrow no doubt he will feel much better.
(i) However she left the room without making a scene.
(j) Well that is the end of the story.

Revision exercise 12 (page 16):

This exercise contains examples of all four kinds of words or groups of words which need to be marked off with commas because they are not absolutely necessary to the meaning of the sentence. Some of the sentences, however, contain groups of words which **are** necessary and they, of course, must **not** be marked off with commas. Write out each sentence, adding commas in the correct places. Do not add any other punctuation.

(a) Well we just could not believe it.
(b) On the tractor sat Farmer Brown happily puffing away at his pipe.

(c)   The Thirty-Nine Steps was a book which he had read and enjoyed several times before.

(d)   The spy is the man wearing the black overcoat.

(e)   He was followed everywhere by his shadow the dog.

(f)   Snatching the old lady's bag he darted away through the crowd.

(g)   However I shall say no more about it.

(h)   There was a slight movement from the furthest curtain behind which the thief was hiding.

(i)   She did her best no doubt but it was not good enough.

(j)   Charles Bailey the father is a much nicer man than Charles Bailey the businessman.

Commas marking off groups of words beginning with *when*, *after*, etc.

Revision exercise 13 (page 18):

Each of the following sentences contains a group of words beginning with *when*, *after*, etc. Write out each sentence, adding commas where necessary. (Some of the sentences will not need any commas.) Do not add any other punctuation.

Example: *Although he had often stolen things he had never been caught until now.*
becomes *Although he had often stolen things, he had never been caught until now.*

(a)   They knew that when their father came home he would be very angry.

(b)   Mrs. Bant went home after she had finished her shopping.

(c)   Before the winter began the squirrels had collected their nuts.

(d)   Because you told me a lie I am punishing you.

(e)   I am punishing you because you told me a lie.

(f) I am afraid that because you told me a lie I shall have to punish you.

(g) They did not surrender until their food ran out.

(h) The plumber said that if he was to do a good job he would need at least a month.

(i) Though he sang as loudly as he could they were still unable to hear him at the back of the hall.

(j) Until he passed his exams he was unable to get a good job.

Other uses of the comma

Revision exercise 14 (page 20):

Write out the following letter, adding commas where necessary. It is a business letter so you must set it out exactly as it is set out here. Do not add any other punctuation (except for three full stops after *Surrey*, *1976* and *Easton*).

5 Green Lane
Blackford
Surrey
26th August 1976

The Manager
Clark's Catering Ltd.
10–15 New Road
Easton

Dear Sir

The Blackford Cricket Club will be holding its usual end-of-season Grand Barbecue on Saturday 18th September. I should be grateful if you would deliver the following goods to the cricket pavilion in Blackford Park Blackford on Friday 17th September:

1800 bread rolls
1200 small sausages
500 beefburgers.

Yours faithfully
Tom Jenkins (Hon. Sec.)

Full stop after abbreviations

Revision exercise 15 (page 23):

Write out the following sentences, adding a full stop after each abbreviated word. Set out addresses correctly, as on the previous page.

Example: *Mr P G Marsh will see you this afternoon at 2 pm.*
becomes *Mr. P. G. Marsh will see you this afternoon at 2 p.m.*

(a)   In this town there are some good hotels, eg the Victoria.
(b)   The first SOS message was received at exactly 2.48 pm.
(c)   Mrs V A Johns, 2 Park St, Bristol.
(d)   Mr and Mrs B D Feather will not be sending Christmas cards this year.
(e)   Miss E Benson, The Old Bakehouse, Hardy Ave, Preston, Lancs.
(f)   Mrs Gould's baby weighed 8 lbs 2 ozs.
(g)   Hamsters, mice, guinea-pigs, etc are all suitable for keeping as pets.
(h)   The Manager, Rentasuit Ltd, 2 Station Rd, Sheffield, Yorks.
(i)   Dr Watts can give you an appointment tomorrow at 5.55 pm.
(j)   The UK joined the EEC in 1975.

General exercises

Revision exercise 16:

There is one mistake in each of the following groups of words. Write out each group of words with the mistake corrected.

(a)   They knew it was too late, they could not win now.

(b) The pop star screamed, shouted, whispered, and sometimes even sang to the audience.

(c) Have you forgotten Mr. Thomas, that you owe me some rent?

(d) "I fell over and cut my knee, sobbed the little boy."

(e) "Where are you going today"? she asked.

(f) The sky, a mass of black clouds told us that there would soon be a storm.

(g) John and Henry who were both scouts, collected the largest amount of money.

(h) However they tried for half an hour to make the television work.

(i) It is possible that the world began about 4,000,0000,00 years ago.

(j) The train arrived exactly at 2.35 pm.

Revision exercise 17:

Write out each of the following sentences, adding only commas where necessary.

(a) The sun's planets are Mercury Venus Earth Mars Jupiter Saturn Uranus Neptune and Pluto.

(b) My dear girl you will come in at ten o'clock or you will not be allowed out at all.

(c) The ball-point pen invented by John Loud in 1888 was developed by two Hungarians Ladisloa and Biro in 1938.

(d) Because they could not agree on the price the sale did not take place.

(e) After Mary had washed her hair she painted her nails.

(f) Over 700000000 people live in China.

(g) If they are to reach Australia and New Zealand by Christmas airmail letters must be posted by Monday 12th December.

(h) The kidnappers did however treat their prisoner kindly.

(i) "Please come home" she begged her son.

(j)   The two boys hitched a lift to Stockholm which is
      the capital of Sweden and stayed there for five
      days.

Revision exercise 18:

Write out the following letter, adding only commas
where necessary.

> 5 Black Horse Rd.
> Whitworth.
> Sunday 15th August 1976.

Dear Mum
   I am having a good time. When I arrived here
everybody made me welcome. Uncle Bill Aunt Susan
Tom and Jane are very friendly and have been very
kind. They have a dog Sadie who is enormous.
However she is a gentle dog and wakes me every
morning by licking my face.
   I wonder thinking of my face whether I left my tooth-
brush toothpaste and face-cloth at home. I can't find
them in my case. Tomorrow we are going to the Mop
the local fair. I shall see you on Friday 21st August.

> With love
> Andrew

Revision exercise 19:

Write out the following sentences, using any of the
punctuation marks you have learned in Books 1, 2 and
3: capital letters, full stop, question mark, exclamation
mark, comma, speech marks and apostrophe.

(a)   breakfast is ready their mother called
(b)   the cat woke up yawned stretched and went back
      to sleep again
(c)   mother he said with tears in his eyes please lie
      down and try to sleep
(d)   because the whole class had worked so hard they
      were all taken to a film before christmas

37

the school will close for the summer holiday on wednesday 19th august at 2.15 pm

(f) unless this shoplifting stops said the manager of the store we shall have to call in the police

(g) she put down her book lost on the moor and looked out of the window

(h) how thoughtless you are christine exclaimed mr west her teacher

(i) the song white christmas written by irving berlin has sold almost 2000000 records

(j) i am sorry said the personnel officer looking at the dirty and badly-dressed young man in front of him but i cannot offer you the job

Revision exercise 20:

Do as you did in revision exercise 19.

(a) mrs lewis asked the postman why he was so late

(b) his new car which was only 1200 cc went extremely fast

(c) the headmistress asked the school do any of you girls know anything about the vandalism which took place on saturday evening

(d) the strongest earthquake ever recorded in the british isles was centred on colchester on 22nd april 1884

(e) swinging silently from branch to branch the gorilla watched jim saunders who was chopping wood in the clearing below

(f) well i think youve made a mistake said hugh

(g) when mr and mrs sinclair arrived in london they went straight to the park hotel

(h) ladies and gentlemen said the prime minister you can trust me

(i) there will be a half-holiday when the school plays its annual match against the old boys on wednesday 13th november

(j) its too difficult said sarah for me to do

Revision exercise 21 :

Do as you did in revision exercise 19.

(a) the united nations organization began on 24th october 1945

(b) dont tell tales tommy scolded his mother

(c) edward iii king of england ruled from 1327 to 1377

(d) vanessa simon and nicola had meanwhile set off down the road to the chip shop

(e) open wider said the dentist and keep still

(f) the fire alarm having sounded at 9.18 am the fire brigade arrived at 9.22 am

(g) What a surprise miss cuthbertson gave her class when she came to school on monday as mrs jackson

(h) dont come near or theyll kill me screamed the hostage

(i) if it doesnt stop raining by midday the match will be cancelled

(j) sandy said quietly if i told you the truth you would not believe it

Revision exercise 22 :

Punctuate the following paragraph, using any of the punctuation marks you have learned in Books 1, 2 and 3: capital letters, full stop, question mark, exclamation mark, comma, speech marks and apostrophe.

excuse me said the nervous-looking man he was carrying a torch and wearing a dark suit which had seen better days yes said the shop assistant he hardly looked up from the magazine which he was reading the man said i bought this torch from you this morning here is the receipt he handed the receipt over the counter yes said the shop assistant well i took the torch home said the man and tried it out when i turned it on the switch just broke off here it is he placed the small silver switch on the counter it must be faulty said the shop assistant that is obvious said the man sharply he was beginning to get cross i should like another torch help yourself said the shop assistant he pointed to the rack where the torches were and went back to his magazine what a shop exclaimed the man as he went over to the torches i shant come here again

Revision exercise 23:

Do as you did in revision exercise 22.

our dog a great dane is called sam he is an intelligent affectionate dog and we are all very fond of him he has however two habits which are especially annoying seeing somebody coming up the path to the front door he will bark loudly and he will always try to get out as soon as we open the door last saturday when i was very busy i heard him barking i knew there must be someone coming up the front path be quiet sam i shouted he stopped barking but when there was a knock on the front door he ran towards it hoping to get out as i opened the door i pushed him away with my foot although it was only a push it must have looked to the man at the door as if i was kicking him the smile went from his face he held out a collecting tin what are you collecting for i asked the RSPCA he replied looking at the dog i was only pushing him away from the door i explained blushing hotly the man said nothing excuse me i muttered i dashed into the kitchen found my purse and went back to the front door the man was looking at sam who was now trotting happily down the front path here you are i said i gave him a pound thank you he said he walked away still not smiling